Emerging
Into
Victory

— COME FORTH —

CHIQUITA CLARK

FOREWORD

Emerging Into Victory, is no ordinary journal. Apostle Chiquita Clark is a phenomenal teacher, preacher and anointed Woman of God. You will find this journal helps to strengthen and empower us to press on as we face the obstacles that come our way in this thing called "life."

I have had the pleasure of knowing Apostle Clark, my sister in Christ, since the fall of 2011. We have built a friendship, kinship and trust for each other, our families and ministries over the years. We are accountability partners and prayer partners who believe that we have been called to be servants of our Most High God.

As you read this journal of how her life has been molded and shaped through adversity, and the highs and lows of parenting, pastoring and being a wife, you will see the fortitude of how Apostle Chiquita was able to emerge into victory. The title of this journal was birthed with a divine call as the pages of the journal tell her story of walking into victory no matter what the obstacles may have been. There were struggles in early ministry when it was extremely difficult for women to preach the gospel. Her guidance and obedience to the elders in her life, has helped her to pen a journal that will be a life changer to many as we rise into the victory that God wants for our lives. No one said it would be easy, but through it all, building a strong and loving relationship with God was well worth the struggle for Apostle Chiquita and she wants each one of us to know that if God can do it for her, He certainly will perform His mighty acts for His children..

Through this journal you will be able to understand that even though things don't look right, you have more bills than money, your children are not listening to you, your marriage is on the rocks, don't quit for your victory lies ahead of you. As Apostle Chiquita reflects back on her small beginnings, her story will catapult you to seek even the more a relationship with God where you will always have a, "I don't understand this but God, You know the plans, now lead and guide me according to Your will and Your way."

As you complete the prayers throughout this journal, you will find that you will no longer look at the negativity of your situation. Our prayer is that this journal will challenge you to walk into your victory. We are praying that you will find love, joy, peace and happiness that will help you understand that through it all, life is worth living. Matthew 19:26 tells us "Jesus looked at them and said to them, "With men this is impossible, but with God all things are possible." Now it's up to you!

In His love,

Apostle Dr. Barbara Maybin Wise, Th.D

INTRODUCTION

If you're reading this book, then that means I finally did it. I've birthed a dream, that is now tangible. Some 10 years later but it has happened. This book was conceived after attending a life changing leadership entrepreneurial conference in Raleigh North Carolina. However, it was prophesied over my life in 2011 by His Eminence Archbishop Harris E. Clark. At that time 2011, I was really experiencing major life challenges, so writing a book was the nowhere on the forefront of my mind. (But it did not mean the assignment had been cancelled). See the book was already within me, but I was in a mental and emotional place of spiritual despair, I could not feel the inspiration to write. But it did not change, what God had predestined for my life. So while attending this conference that Friday night the guest speaker, spoke on the "Orphan Spirit" which can lead us into a place of despair and despondency. She called an altar call and I found myself on my knees crying out to

God to help me. I knew He was my Father, and I was not an orphan.

However, I needed a breakthrough like I had never experienced before. Maybe you have never experienced what seems like waves of disappointments, hurts and discouragement; and before you can catch your breath another something hits you. Well, that was me. Yes me, the preacher, the leader, the encourager you know the one who can hype, motivate and pray everyone else through, but herself. I needed help, and I knew deep within, that only GOD could deliver the help I so desperately needed.

I'm not sure how long the I was at the altar, I lost myself in prayer and I made my mind up, before going down on my knees, that I would not leave until I felt the releasing within my heart and spirit. You know Breakthrough!!! The determination like Jacob had, I won't let you go Lord until you bless my soul.

See I had been guilty of operating in a type of False Humility. What I mean is the Lord, wanted me to spearhead this new assignment, but I was so focused on surviving that I was unaware becoming a victim of rejection, and because of the past hurts and disappointments, I was mentally and spiritually shutting down. That's why I am so grateful for my husband Bruce Clark, he kept me covered in prayer, when I could not pray for myself. Whether you're married or not always have an accountability partner that can pray and know how to speak life into spirit. (They won't judge you) they will just love you through it. (Thank you Bae)

Maybe you, are somewhat like me unknowingly have fallen prey to the cares of life the hits and blows has knocked the breath out of you. I need for you to keep reading, because "It's NOT Over" if God did it for me (and He did) guess what, He will do for you, but YOU have got to want it.

Over the next few chapters in this book, I want to share with you how, I found my fire and passion back for my life and the works in which I was predestined to do. Remember, I told you about being at the altar, well I heard these words very clear, "Chiquita it's time to Emerge Beyond this place. Emerge from the fears, doubts, frustration and disappointment. It's time to come from the shadows into view" Emerge Beyond and help others just like you to come to the forefront.

DEDICATION

I give All the Glory, Honor and Praise to my Heavenly Father, without Him, I am nothing. But because of Him I am. He has given me this awesome opportunity and for that I'm so humbled and grateful. I am not ashamed of the gospel of Jesus Christ and acknowledging Him as my Lord and Savior.

To my amazing husband of 37years Bishop Bruce Clark, I love you and I'm so grateful that God blessed me to have you. You are my biggest supporter and encourager. Thank you for praying for me, cooking for us whenever my schedule was on overload. (You never complained). You always encourage me to obey the Lord, even when I sometimes struggle to grasp what I heard. I love you forever Bae!!!

To my birth children Jamarrea and Mariah, when I look at you, I'm constantly reminded of the miraculous healing power of God. When the doctors told me, that I would never be able to conceive, the Lord had another plan in the works. (He opened my womb with you) and I love you, and I'm so proud of you, and the comeback tenacity that you both carry. Don't ever give in to the enemy. Too my other two children Garrust and Ryshell both of which I love as if I birthed you and I'm proud of your accomplishments in life as well. There's no limit to your blessings.

To Archbishop Harris E. Clark and Lady Betty Clark, thank you for the love, impartation and support you have extended over the years. Bishop, you prophesied this book over my life in 2011 well it's ten year later, but God is faithful to His Word. Thank you and Elect Lady for your love, wisdom and prayers, I'm forever grateful for you both and KLFII family.

Restoration Worship Center, the greatest church on this side of heaven (in my opinion) I cannot begin to express my gratitude for your genuine willingness to go above and beyond the call of duty in assisting me to answering the call and fulfilling the assignment. I Love you all BIG!!!

To Apostle Cheryle Bush and Apostle Barbara Wise, thank you two ladies for Pushing me, Praying with me and for me. Encouraging me not to get comfortable and lovingly keeping me grounded in handling the pressures of life. Tina Moore, with Tina Moore Global, I still hear your voice, "there are millions waiting on you, yes you Chiquita Clark" The Push has caused a greater yearning of determination within me, to Win. I love each of you and I'm so thankful for you.

SPECIAL DEDICATIONS

To my momma Dora Drinkard, who went to live with the Lord 6/25/2021, I miss you and I thank you for all that you instilled in me. You always told, me Gladys and Jermaine, (My siblings) don't do anything halfway, give it your all. We're still giving it our all mom. Sleep in Peace my love, someday we will meet you in glory. Oh, and by the way, we are taking care of Poppa Carl, but you were right sometimes he can be really stubborn. (LOL)

To my dad William Ravenell, who went to live with the Lord on 5/28/18, I miss you Pops, and of course being the oldest child. I think I am running things, just like you would want me too (LOL) We're making sure GrandNella is good, and I've got Aunt Cille as my back up security. Rest in Peace, one day we will see you again.

CHAPTER ONE

Busy but Not Fulfilled

So, I love people! I am an extrovert, my husband says, you will strike up a conversation with a tree. All my life I've enjoyed talking to people even as a child I would be the one who got in trouble for talking while the teacher was talking. I always knew my report was going to have the same note, "Chiquita is doing great, she just needs to work on not talking so much." I've learned to control it better over the years. Maybe, because I finally figured out. God gave me a voice and a gift to converse with people. Being a person with an extrovert personality can sometimes get me into trouble, because as I meet people, many are hurting, and others are looking for answers. And I find myself trying to help them, find and answer to their problems. Lending a helping hand is something we was taught being reared as children. What I didn't know was, sometime people don't really want your help, they want you to wait on them. In doing so, this process can sometimes have you so busy that you're not fulfilled, because you tired.

While serving in ministry, with my husband. We serve as pastors to a wonderful church family Restoration Anointed Worship Center in Lavonia, Georgia. I was serving in my own ministry as well as travelling out to preach and teach the gospel. After the service, I would feel so empty. I knew something, wasn't right within me. How can I see all these people get blessed and witness the power of God so mighty and then once, I get in my car, I felt so lonely and empty? It's not enough to go through the motion, I'm reminder of the scripture in *1ˢᵗ Corinthians 9:27 "But I keep my own body under subjection: lest that by any means, when I have preached to others, I myself should be a castaway"*.

I did not want to miss the mark after I seen others receive their breakthroughs from the same word that I'm preaching and teaching from. What's wrong with me? Am I Not Enough?

Today I leave Insufficient, and I Emerge into I Am Enough:

I decree and declare that because I Am fearfully and wonderfully made. I Am created in the likeness and image of the Almighty God; therefore, I renounce every lie that the enemy will whisper against my life and destiny in Jesus name.

Write your prayer: _____

_____

_____

_____

_____

_____

_____

_____

_____

_____

_____

_____

_____

_____

_____

_____

_____

_____

_____

Always remember that just because one can be seen as busy does not necessarily mean that they're being fulfilled. Sometimes it's our way of not having to think about all the things that I should be doing. Blocking out the mental fear of stepping out on faith. After coming into my realization that ministry was my pacifier, I made a conscience decision to make sure that the works, in which I was doing was making a godly impact within the lives of others. In other words, making sure that my labor was not in vain, and that I was not looking to be validated by the opinion of others. Throughout reading this book, take the time to reflect and allow the Holy Spirit to reveal to you, areas in which you may have been or may be, guilty of just being busy. I'm not talking about being a busy body, no, that's something totally different. This type of busyness is where you throw yourself into something that in actuality, it was never meant for you.

You assigned yourself to the tasks, and now you're tired and somewhat weary. So, what am I supposed to do you may ask? Well, I'm glad you asked; according to the scriptures, you will find on several occasion varies individuals inquired of the Lord.

"Inquiring of the Lord" this is our key to fulfillment. Spend time in prayer and meditation concerning that which weighs on your heart. (Whether it's your family, health, finances, relationships, business, or careers) surrender it over to the Lord, and He will direct you in the way in which you should go.

Isaiah 58:11

And the Lord shall guide the continually, and satisfy thy soul in drought, and make fat thy bones: and thy shall be like a watered garden, and like a spring of water, whose waters fail not.

Be encouraged as you step into your New Place of Being Fulfilled!

CHAPTER TWO

Follow the Instructions

As I stated earlier, my husband and I attended this conference in Raleigh North Carolina. The conference theme was entitled: New Now Next. What I didn't tell you is that I knew absolutely "no one" at this conference but my husband. However, in attempting to talk myself from registering us for this conference, a yearning was within me, that we should attend. After laying my mental fleece out umpteenth time, I registered us and made the hotel reservations. I had no idea that God was setting me up to set me free. Sometimes, God will put in a room with total strangers and the only thing you have in common is a kindred spirit. That's how I knew we was in the right place.

When I say that the atmosphere was charged with High Expectations. Whew!!!

I was not the only one, longing for God to revive them, having a need to be refreshed and fire to be reignited. I was in a New surrounding with New people that had a Now hunger a Now thirst in order to excel into their Next. It was a divine setup.

Like me someone reading this, is in a place where you need to move from among that and those who are so familiar to you. Maybe just a weekend, maybe a permanent move. My point is this, your level of clarity becomes clearer when you have something different in view. When you're among likeminded people that wants to embrace their vision with actions, not just hanging around talking about it. What I'm about to say, may be a little intimidating, but surround yourself with people who are great at what it is that you desire to do. Follow them on their social media platforms. If they have books, videos etc... buy the books and READ them watch the videos. If it's possible, ask them if you can take them out to lunch. It will be the best lunch money you have spent in quite a while. Why? Because you're absorbing knowledge while you're in their presence.

I heard many stories that sounded like mind, but I also heard the words of breakthrough, confidence, and wake your successful self-up. I heard speaker after speaker, address the barriers that had me trapped, but thanks be to God who gives us the Victory. The walls came crashing down. I'm so glad that I obeyed the instructions to attend this conference. I left all my fears, doubt, opinion of man and the lies the enemy had tried to convince me, that there was no more to receive or believe God for. A wonderful change had come over me, from the inside out. And because God has no respect of person, you too, can be healed, delivered, and set free.

When the world says
Give up.
Hope whispers...
Try it one more time

Today I leave Doubt and I Emerge into Confident

I decree and declare that I am confident to this very thing, He who has begun a good work within me shall perform it, until the day of Jesus Christ.

Write your prayer: _____

_____

_____

_____

_____

_____

_____

_____

_____

CHIQUITA CLARK

CHAPTER THREE

Submerge Into Prayer and Worship

There's nothing like being in the presence of the Lord, especially during your personal prayer time. But when you find it hard to pray yourself, but you're determined to get your breakthrough. Oh, my goodness, submerging into that place of feeling like no one is in the room, but you and God. That's exactly what happened to me while I was at the altar that Friday night. I think I cried from a depth in my soul that I didn't know existed. Anyways, I just know whenever, I heard the words "It's time to Emerge from this place" those words resonated within my spirit to the point, that it literally felt like someone had awaken me out of a deep sleep. And the truth be told, that's what happened. The enemy was trying to smother My spiritual passion and desires out.

See if the enemy can smother your faith and put a constant reminder before you of how hard life is, and where is your God now. He will have you convinced that God no longer cares. That's why is a good thing to connect yourself with strong bible faith believers. Also learn the word of God and write out your decrees and declarations. Say what the Word of God says and shut down the voice of the enemy.

Listening to Praise and Worship music will sooth your mind and bring your spirit in a peaceful place to hear the voice of the Lord. Don't worry about how you sound when you pray. You need to be uniquely you. Some people want to sound like someone they heard in church pray. Just open your mouth and start talking to the Lord with a sincere heart. After all He knows all about us; and there's nothing hidden from Him. Even that, that you have held in your heart, that was contrary to His will concerning your life. I tell you the Lord is faithful.

Jeremiah 33:3 is one of my favorite scriptures

Call upon me and I will answer you and I will show you great and mighty things that you didn't know.

I received my breakthrough that night and my perspectives on life has changed dramatically. I'm determined to do and be all that God has created me for. I hope you are feeling a reawakening of the gifts and potentials that has been dormant coming to life again. There is greatness on the inside of you, and there are people waiting for you to deliver. Often, we are so tunnel minded that we put limits on God and on how we think He chooses to use us for His glory. What I mean is this, several of you that will read this book, already know what you need to be doing. But because it's not churchy and you have become paralyzed by religion. Listen being able to minister is not limited to the church house alone. No, we are called to serve in the marketplace, the government, our family, educational arenas, media platforms, arts & entertainment, and the church. (The Seven Mountains of Influence).

My prayer for you today is that as you spend quality time in prayer and meditation with the Lord that He will be a lamp unto your feet and will make your pathway bright.

Today I leave Prayerlessness and I Emerge into Praying in His Presence

I decree and declare that God desire for me to spend time with Him. According to James 4:8a If I draw close to God, He will draw close to me.

Write your prayer: _____

_____

_____

_____

_____

_____

_____

_____

CHAPTER FOUR

The Emerging Transformation

Let's talk about the process. This where most people will throw in the towel or just walk away. No one wants to go through the duration of the process. But can I tell you it is much needed in order to get you to your next. We are living in a time where people want what they want, when they want it, they don't like having to wait. You know they're from the microwaveable crew, the In-sta-tonians (LOL) Just because someone attained something quick fast and, in a hurry, does not necessarily mean it's of quality; nor does it mean that you need to do it right away if at all. After receiving my breakthrough, and my word of clarity, I still needing guidance on how to move forward with what I knew.

Being full of zeal and no directions, can be devasting. So, I continued to glean from the services. On Saturday morning, while browsing the vendors areas. I saw a banner that stood out to me, spoke with the instructor for more in-depth information, concerning the program. I knew this was the answer. Although, I was in ministry preaching to many, within the congregation, what about the ones that attended a different church, yet they were drawn to me. They didn't need me to be their pastor, they needed me as their life coach. Someone who would put pressure on them to unlock their gifts. Their pastors needed the gifts to help with the ministry. I didn't sign up for the program right away, but I stay in the loop of several active coaches. In November 2018 I gave myself an early birthday gift. I invested in myself by enrolling into the coaching program. There's no greater investment, you can give yourself than that of knowledge. I became a Professional Certified Life Coach & Mentor. I wish I could tell you that it was over-night success with ease. Wrong answer, it was work. I had to show up on live social media platforms with something worth while to say, not just preaching a message. This was not that, but I could not give up. It felt strange saying I'm a Life Coach and what I do is? See people knew me from the ministry, and would call or text me about whatever they had going on, asking for prayer, or an encouraging word.

But what they didn't know was now, I'm able to determine in a greater way whether or not you need the preacher, the coach or if you're just taking up time, making excuses.

Now we are in a brand-new year 2019, and the transformation to change, be and do is getting real to me. I worked in corporate for 32 years and I absolutely love my job as a Member Services Representative. I was constantly dealing with people. From contractors, homeowners, tenants, engineers and even the downright mean and hateful ones. Still accommodating people was my happy place. That was until there was a discontentment that left me feeling unappreciated and undervalued. Now that I look back over it, it was a God move.

God knew my loyalty to the company would be a hinderance to my loyalty to Him, so I believe He provokes us to the point of making us make a move or be miserable staying in a place. I begin to pray, and I ask the Lord to let my husband know first, as to when I could off my corporate job. Although my flesh was ready immediately, the transformation process was still in progress.

(Wait I say on the Lord)

One Sunday during our church service, my husband was preaching and in the middle of his message, he looked at me and said, the spirit of Lord says you can retire early off your job. He's going to take care of us. I broke down in tears, because my husband didn't know what I had asked the Lord for in my prayer time. In September 2019, I wrote my resignation letter to retire on years of service out. I had to intended to retire on my work anniversary, in October, there again, the Lord had another plan in mind. The company needed me to help prepare someone for my position. It ended up that I didn't retire until the latter part of December. And then.......

2020 Pandemic hits

Today I evict Doubt and I Emerge into Trusting the Lord

I decree and declare that I will trust in the Lord and lean not to my own understanding, I will acknowledge Him and He will direct my path.

Write your prayer: _____

_____

_____

_____

_____

_____

_____

_____

_____

_____

_____

_____

_____

_____

_____

_____

_____

_____

_____

CHAPTER FIVE

Going Forward

Although 2020 Pandemic was something the most of us had never experienced, it was also a time that should have caused us to appreciate life and one another. I experienced the heart wrenching pain of losing very special loved ones, but I also learned how to Be Still and Know. What do you do when you can't change the diagnosis, the projected timeframe of someone taking their final breath? For me, I found a new strength in the Lord. I cried, I prayed, I may have even pleaded, but the final say was ultimately up to the Lord. With that understanding, I begin praying Lord, give me Peace.

Philippians 4:7 And the peace of God, which passeth all understanding, shall keep your hearts and minds through Christ Jesus

I found the peace of God, doesn't mean you agree with His decision, but rather you respect the fact that He is an All-knowing God. The whole world is basically paralyzed and yet God gives me instructions to move forward. In moving forward, I continued to gain insight and information. Faith without works is dead (James 2:26b) In life we must learn to persevere through our trials. Remember earlier, we I talked about the quick fix people? Well, I've learned over the years that you never come out at same pace from each. God will develop something greater in you while purging everything that can't go into your next.

I've been guilty of trying to take people with me, and God didn't give them the invitation to go. Maybe, it's the excitement, or not having to go alone, whichever way, don't assume it's you plus one. He may be calling you, just you, party of one.

The assignments, business ventures, or doors of opportunities that I have may not fit you, and vice versa, yours may not fit me. But what we can do is this, cheer each other on and celebrate the giftings that God has placed inside of you for His Glory.

The peace that only God can give you for the journey is so amazing. Get up it's time to Go Be Great!!

Impossible

Or

I'm-Possible

Today I leave being passive, and I Emerge into Confidence

I decree and declare that I because I trust in the Lord and I seek His instructions, I can great things, with the help of the Lord.

Write your prayer: _____

_____

_____

_____

_____

_____

_____

_____

_____

_____

_____

_____

_____

_____

_____

_____

_____

_____

_____

_____

CHAPTER SIX

I Found Me Again

As I think on this chapter, I smile BIG!! And so should you. I found me, say it with me, "I Found Me". Now the only way this statement make sense is that you and I had to be lost from somewhere, right? Right! I wasn't lost doing worldly things, quite the opposite. I was lost in the shuffle of religion. Yep, you read that right. This chapter will be a little longer okay. Let me explain, I was the first female to be ordained as a minister in my home church, so I needed and wanted to make sure that I was doing ministry perfect. I remember telling my pastor that I felt the call of God on my life. He probably knew it before me, but at that time 1995 very few women were being licensed especially in the Baptist church. But Rev. Mayweather was receptive, and he said to me, "if God has called you, who am I to hold you back. He passed the information on to the deacon board and a date was scheduled for me to give my initial sermon.

May 14, 1995, I delivered my first message entitled, "The Lord Is My Shepherd" It was also Mother's Day, I was so nervous, but I truly thank the Lord, for speaking through me on that day. I delivered the message the way God gave it to me, I received my license certification and at that time, it didn't dawn on me that I had made history and become a new trailblazer for women preachers. My spiritual mother Apostle Classie Green, taught me the female version of pulpit etiquettes. And to never be offended if I'm not offered an opportunity to partake during a service if it was predominantly all male preachers present. I followed her instructions, and then on one occasion I was asked to fill-in, to give a word of prayer. My Lord, and the power of God fell in the room. I found my voice, I found my identity, I knew, I had and assignment to serve God's people, again what God didn't tell me was; he was going to uproot me and my family from our home church and send us to another church. But He did!! (This was part of God's plan and training for my future).

Six years serving under the leadership of Bishop Danny Hughes at the Hartwell Church of God of Prophecy. We received, not one, not two but three prophetic words, that the Lord was moving us to begin our own ministry. Having served as the assistant pastor to Bishop Hughes, being a lead pastor was not on my itinerary. However, April 2001, we held our first service as Restoration Anointed Worship and Praise Center, with 6 adults and about 8 children.

And although I understood the assignment, does not mean opposition will not come, the enemy is so cunning, and if he can shut you up and shut you down that's exactly what he will do. And that's what the enemy tried on so many levels. Whereas I'm married with a family, I'm pastoring, and I have a full-time corporate job. I felt like I was in isolation. The questionings within myself, did I really hear God back in 1995? Was this a fabricated religious idea that I dreamt up? If this was God, why did I feel so alone? These were the battles that I faced daily by myself. Mind you, my husband is very supportive, but he did not have the answers for what I, said I heard God say to me. So, during the span of a 10-year period in this place, (my personal isle of Patmos) I along with my husband, experienced, bankruptcy, wage garnishment, back-to-back deaths of family members, children getting in trouble, health issues, foreclosure and a grandchild being born as a preemie at 1lb9oz.

When all you have is the Word of God, I found that it was all that I needed. I kept preaching and teaching the word of God, while behind the scenes, no one really knew the struggles. I didn't look like what I had been through. And the key word is "through". You may be in a hard place as you're reading this book right now, but take courage my friend, you will get through it. In 2011, we lost our home, and despite all the heartaches and disappointments, there were many fond memories made as well. The assignment didn't change. I still had a charge to serve the people of God both inside and outside the church. How will they know that God is a restorer unless something falls apart? (In this case it seemed as if it was our entire lives) You guess it, November 2014, the Lord had restored us back with our own home, credit was restored, family restored and now mentally and spiritually I now feel so restored and empowered. My testimony of God's Grace, and His Restoring Power was so personal.

People need to not only hear the preached word, but they also needed to see the word in demonstration. They needed a modern-day Christian, preacher, teacher person to show up on the outside of the four walls of the church building. Some of my clients will tell me, I know what the bible says, but what I need is for someone to help me to put it into motion in my life. Or I know what to do, I just don't know how to do it.

After my encounter in Raleigh North Carolina, I realized that I had allowed traditions, the opinion of others, fear and uncertainly to limit myself from excelling forward. But I found me. I found out that I can serve others in more than one area. I found that I have a voice, and that it's needed for the nations, it's needed in the marketplace, it's needed in the educational sector, as well as to that those who feel as if they have nothing to offer. I'm here to encourage you and to help you to reawaken the gifts and potentials on the inside of you that has laid dormant. It's time for you to Emerge. Emerge come into view with your purpose and destiny. Stop procrastinating and trying to push it off onto someone else. This is your designated moment. You have been called for such a time as this.

And I say to you, it's your time to show up unapologetically. It doesn't matter that you can't do it like someone else. That's a good thing, because I'm uniquely me and you are you. What good is it to have a gift, but never open the box. You can admire the wrapping paper, but never experience the actual gift. The same is true with your gift, the gift that resides on the inside of you is needed in the earth.

There are people waiting on you, to just show up.

Today I leave Obscurity and I Emerge into Visibility

I decree and declare that I am no longer in the shadows of doubt and fear but am emerging into my new place of living life more abundantly.

Write your prayer: _____

_____

_____

_____

_____

_____

_____

_____

CHIQUITA CLARK

CHAPTER SEVEN

Now that I'm Here?

I'm so glad that you're still reading with me. I have just a little more to share with you, okay? Two of my most favorite scriptures are below. Let's look at them. The first one is:

Philippians 1:6 Being confident of this very thing, that he which hath begun a good work in you will perform it until the day of Jesus Christ

And the second one is:

1ˢᵗ Corinthians 2:9 But it is written, eye hath not seen, nor ear heard, neither have entered the heart of man, the things which God hath prepared for them that love Him.

Please sir, please ma'am, take time to read those scriptures one more time.

Do you see it? Do you see the promises that are activated in those scriptures for your life? Once the gifts that you are carrying are reawaken and nourished, your confidence restored you should rest in the power and ability of our creator. Our Heavenly Father. (Abba Father) And then, there's a direct spoken word to you and me as God lovers.

It is already written out, no other eyes have seen it, no other ears have heard, no other heart has received to do it the way God gives it to you to do. See it doesn't matter how many other people are in the same line of business. Your unique style will draw those who has been predestined for you. I have learned, just follow the instructions from the Lord, and He will send the people, the customers, and the clients. And here's the thing, it's not always who we may think it will be. Take the limits off God, He is a Limitless God. Can I encourage your faith for just a moment? He is the same God that helped you through that last place of uncertainty, you thought you couldn't get through. And when you look back over your life, you can't help but see the hand of God working on your behalf over and over and over again.

Hebrews 13:8 Jesus Christ is the same yesterday, today and forever.

Maybe, you have procrastinated about going back to school, starting up that business, or maybe you talked yourself out from applying for the position on your job. And maybe, just maybe, because of past failures and disappointments, you now settle, not that you are content, you just settle to avoid the emotional and mental frustration. Now that you have read this book to this point, I pray that you're enlighten and have a better understanding of warring through adversity.

Getting a "No" is not always a bad thing.

Sometimes No is No, because this is going to hurt you in the long run. Or No, not right now, you need to mature in some areas, and then it's No, because what I have in store for you, is so much greater than this.

What I need for you to do is this? Get started doing something with your gifts and abilities. Start doing something that beneficial for bettering yourself. After all this should be personal to you.

#itspersonal

Today I leave behind Procrastination, and I embrace Emerging Forward

I decree and declare, that I can do all things through Christ who gives me the strength.

Write your prayer: _____

_____

_____

_____

_____

_____

_____

_____

_____

_____

_____

_____

_____

_____

_____

_____

_____

_____

_____

_____

AFFIRMATIONS AND DECLARATIONS

Speak the following affirmations and declarations over your family and yourself as often as you need to.

I decree and declare that great and mighty is the Lord my God, who heals me from sickness, disease and infirmities. By the stripes that Jesus bared on Calvary's cross, with His stripes, I declare I am Healed.

This is the day that the Lord and has made and I will rejoice and be glad in it. Out of His holy mountain He has heard my cry.

Because the Lord is my shepherd and will supply my every need, I do not fear begin in lack or want. The Lord is El 'Shaddai the all sufficient God, the God who is more than enough. He makes me lay in green pastures and leads me beside the quite streams.

I am made in the likeness and image of the almighty God; therefore, I declare that I am fearfully and wonderfully made. I bind my mind to the mind of Christ Jesus, and I think on the things that are honest, just, pure, lovely and of good report.

I decree and declare that every generational curse paternal and maternal is broken and destroyed off my life and out of my bloodline. I plead the blood of Jesus over my children, my grandchildren and their children. I declare that they shall fulfill their God given assignments sweatless.

I decree and declare that no weapon formed against me shall prosper. I declare that the weapons will malfunction, misfire and automatically disengage itself, In Jesus name.

Father, in the name of Jesus,

I declare you're holy, you're righteous, you are the great I Am and there is none like you. You are the only true and living God, and I worship you. I come before you in prayer, thanking you for saving my soul and receiving me as your very own.

Thank you for always being close and giving me peace when the chaos of life tries to overwhelm me. Thank you for every struggle and battle, it was there that I learn to trust you and to see you in a new way. Without you Father, I can do nothing, but because of you, I can do all things as you give me the strength. Be thy glorified, in the life that I live, and, in the service, I give, that the world may see You high and lifted up.

In Jesus Name Amen

CONCLUSION

As we come to the end in this little book, it is my prayer that the contents have a huge impact on your life now and forever. Continue to reflect on these pages and the prayers you wrote, down, especially when no one is around to encourage you. You now have your own words to encourage yourself. May you be strengthened by the Word of the Lord, engulfed by His Presence and Empowered with His Glory. I'm here cheering you on, God believes in you, I believe in you, and I want You to believe in yourself as you trust in the Lord.

Amazing child of God, Emerge into Your Place of Victory.

Today I release Anxiousness and I Emerge into the Peace of God that calms All my fears and anxieties.

Write your prayer: _____

_____

_____

_____

_____

_____

_____

_____

_____

_____

_____

_____

_____

_____

_____

_____

_____

_____

Today I let go of Fear of Failure and I Emerge into my Winning Season

Write your prayer and declaration:

_____

_____

_____

_____

_____

_____

_____

_____

_____

_____

_____

_____

_____

_____

_____

_____

_____

_____

_____

I Can, I Will and I am Emerging into My Victory

Write out your goals:

Goal #1.

_____

_____

_____

_____

Goal #2.

_____

_____

_____

_____

Goal #3.

_____

_____

_____

_____

For booking information, please visit our
website at www.chiquitaclark.com

Like our page on Facebook Emerging Beyond

Instagram: emerging_beyond

Or email us at chiquitaclark84@gmail.com

www.ingramcontent.com/pod-product-compliance
Lightning Source LLC
LaVergne TN
LVHW022013080426
835513LV00009B/697